Ready, Steady, Practise!

Laura Griffiths

Grammar & Punctuation
Pupil Book **Year 4**

Features of this book

- Clear explanations and worked examples for each grammar and punctuation topic from the KS2 National Curriculum.

- Questions split into three sections that become progressively more challenging:

- 'How did you do?' checks at the end of each topic for self-evaluation.

- Regular progress tests to assess pupils' understanding and recap on their learning.

- Answers to every question in a pull-out section at the centre of the book.

Contents

Nouns – singular and plural	4
Apostrophes	6
Was or were?	8
Did or done?	10
Noun phrases 1	12
Noun phrases 2	14
Progress test 1	16
Paragraphs	18
Fronted adverbials 1	20
Fronted adverbials 2	22
Pronouns 1	24
Pronouns 2	26
Determiners and articles	28
Progress test 2	30
Direct speech 1	32
Direct speech 2	34
Standard and non-standard English	36
Full stops, exclamation marks and question marks	38
Proof reading	40
Progress test 3	42
Answers (centre pull-out)	1–4

Nouns – singular and plural

Nouns can either be **singular** or **plural.** Singular means one. Plural means more than one.

A **regular** plural noun ends in **s** or **es**.

Sometimes a plural noun can be **irregular** and not end in **s** or **es**.

Examples:

Regular

Singular	Plural
girl	girls
class	classes

Irregular

Singular	Plural
person	people
man	men

An apostrophe is used to show possession of a singular or plural noun. This is when something belongs to someone or something.

Example:

Singular	Plural
The dog's basket	The dogs' basket

Warm up

1) Find all the **plural** nouns in each sentence below.

   a) The cows were in the field.

   b) The excited astronauts were trying on their new spacesuits.

   c) We are going to the library to listen to stories.

   d) The cats and dogs were making lots of noise because they were frightened of the loud fireworks.

   e) We have sandwiches, crisps, apples and sweets in our picnic today.

   f) There were lots of people waiting at the platform for the next two trains this morning.

Test yourself

2 Write the **irregular plural** for each of these nouns.

a)
woman

b)
child

c)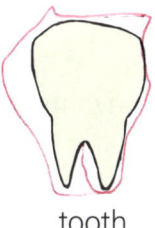
tooth

d)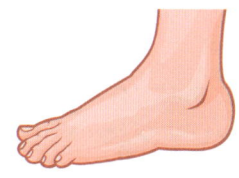
foot

Challenge yourself

3 Rewrite the sentences below and use the nouns from the box to fill in the gaps. If you need to, change the noun to its plural so that the sentence makes sense.

| friend | goose | tail | teacher | dog |

a) Yesterday the _____ said I tried really hard in maths.
b) I have three _____ who all live near to my house.
c) When _____ are happy they wag their _____.
d) The ducks and _____ were swimming in the pond.

How did you do?

Apostrophes

An **apostrophe** is used to show **contraction**: when letters are missed out to join two words.

> **Examples:**
> do not ⟶ don't   I have ⟶ I've   it is ⟶ it's

An **apostrophe** is also used to show **possession**: when something belongs to something else.

If the owner is **singular**, add an apostrophe followed by an **s** to the end of the word.

> **Examples:**
> Matt**'s** lunch   Amita**'s** book   the day**'s** events

If the owner is **plural**, and the word ends in **s**, just add an apostrophe after the s.

> **Examples:**
> the boys**'** lunch   the girls**'** books   the days**'** events

If the owner is **plural** but the word does **not** end in **s**, it is an irregular word. Treat it as if it were singular and add an apostrophe followed by an **s**.

> **Examples:**
> the children**'s** lunchboxes   the men**'s** books   the women**'s** events

Warm up

1 Copy and complete the tables below.

Full words	Contraction
can not	can't
would not	
	isn't
you are	
	we've

Full words	Contraction
I am	
	let's
	we're
I will	
	they'd

Test yourself

2 Rewrite these sentences using an apostrophe and the letter **s** where necessary.

a) Toms jumper is too small for him.

b) The giraffes neck is very long.

c) The mens toilets are out of order.

d) This is Daniels coat.

e) Mrs Javaid class are going on a school trip today.

f) The girl pencil case was green.

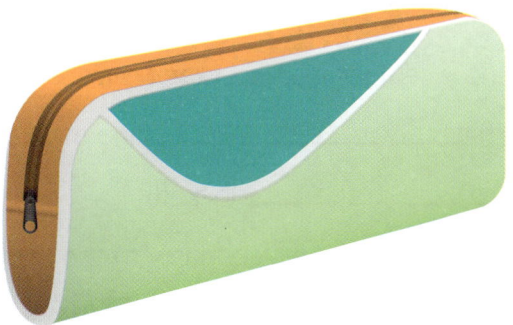

Challenge yourself

3 Using an apostrophe, contract the words. Then use each contracted word in a short sentence.

a) it is

b) you have

c) did not

d) I will

How did you do?

7

Was or were?

Many mistakes in grammar are because the verb and the noun are not matched correctly.

For instance, sometimes **was** and **were** get muddled.

As a rule, if the subject is **singular** use **was**, except when the subject is **you**.

If the subject is **plural**, or the word **you** is used, put **were**.

Examples:

Singular	Plural	You (singular or plural)
He **was** happy.	They **were** happy.	You (the boy) **were** happy.
The boy **was** happy.	The boys **were** happy.	You (the boys) **were** happy.

Warm up

1 Copy and complete these sentences using **was** or **were**.

a) Rebecca and Varsha _____ baking a cake.

b) The school gate _____ locked.

c) The wicked witch _____ nasty to the frog.

d) You _____ very cross!

e) The cars _____ stuck in a traffic jam.

f) It _____ her ballet exam last week.

Test yourself

2 Choose **was** or **were** to fill each gap in the story so that it is written correctly.

Once upon a time there
a) _____ a lion lying by a tree. A little mouse
b) _____ running up and down the lion's back and he
c) _____ beginning to make the lion angry. The lion turned its large head and opened its mouth widely. With its piercing eyes glaring, the lion
d) _____ about to swallow the little mouse in one big gulp.

Just then, the little mouse squeaked, "Please don't eat me! One day you might need me to help you."

The lion laughed but let the little mouse go free. He
e) _____ sure he would never need help from such a small, pathetic creature. Then, one day, three men
f) _____ walking through the forest holding nets. The men
g) _____ trying to catch the lion and swiftly threw a net over the lion's strong body. The lion roared and struggled but there
h) _____ nothing he could do. He could not escape.

Just then, the little mouse returned to help the lion. He began, very slowly, to gnaw and chew through the net with his sharp teeth. Eventually, the mouse made a hole that
i) _____ wide enough for the lion to escape.

Challenge yourself

3 Choose the correct word to start each question.

a) **Was / Were** the girls playing tennis last night?

b) **Was / Were** it cold on the way to school this morning?

c) **Was / Were** there any sweets left in the bag?

d) **Was / Were** the television left on?

How did you do?

Did or done?

Sometimes **did** and **done** get muddled. The words **has**, **have** or **had** should normally appear before **done**. The examples in the table below should help you.

Examples:

Past tense	Present perfect tense	Past perfect tense
I **did** it.	I **have done** it.	I **had done** it.
You **did** it.	You **have done** it.	You **had done** it.
He / she / it **did** it.	He / she / it **has done** it.	He / she / it **had done** it.
We **did** it.	We **have done** it.	We **had done** it.
They **did** it.	They **have done** it.	They **had done** it.

Warm up

1) Write out the correct form of the verb in each sentence.

   a) They **done** / **did** it together.

   b) Ella had **did** / **done** very well in her badminton match.

   c) I **did** / **done** all my homework.

   d) They **done** / **did** the cooking together.

Test yourself

2 Choose **did** or **done** to fill each gap in the following sentences.

a) What _____ you buy from the shops?

b) They've _____ very well.

c) We've _____ the painting carefully.

d) _____ you catch the bus or the train?

e) We've _____ all our activities.

f) I _____ my best!

Challenge yourself

3 Match the correct ending to the start of each sentence.

a) I have done — very well in their swimming lesson.

b) We did — a handstand together.

c) They did — all my homework!

4 Write two sentences of your own using **did** and **done** correctly.

How did you do?

11

Noun phrases 1

A **phrase** is a small group of words that makes up a meaningful unit in a sentence.

A noun phrase does not usually have a verb and it does not make sense on its own.

Examples:

The rubbish was put **in the bin**.

The fish were swimming **around the pond**.

Often a single noun could replace a phrase. Noun phrases are used to add more detail.

Example:

The **lucky little girl** won a prize.

In the example above, this could simply have said, "The girl won a prize." The words "lucky little" add more detail.

Warm up

1 What word type is **not** usually found in a noun phrase? Choose from the words below.

verb   noun   adjective   adverb

Test yourself

2 Find the noun phrase in each of these sentences.

a) My friend's cat likes jumping.

b) We ate dinner in the kitchen.

c) I drank a cup of warm tea.

d) Alex ran along the beach.

e) Kara's pink bedroom was messy.

f) He walked down the path.

g) We can't go shopping in the heavy rain.

Challenge yourself

3 Copy the sentences and choose a noun phrase below to complete each one.

of dirty plates	at the park	after lunch
deep and cold	upside down	small and quiet

a) Bats hang …

b) The waiter was carrying a pile …

c) The mouse, …, scuttled away.

d) The sea is …

e) We played football …

f) Bo finished his homework …

4 Read the noun phrase at the start of each sentence and write a suitable ending.

a) After a long time, …

b) The pretty, white snowflakes …

How did you do?

13

Noun phrases 2

Phrases are a small group of words (or just one word) that form part of a sentence. Using adjectives can expand noun phrases and tell us more about the noun.

Noun phrases have a noun (or pronoun) as the main word.

> **Examples:**
>
> shoes   the shoes   the old pair of shoes
>
> me   silly old me

Prepositional phrases begin with a preposition and are followed by a noun phrase.

> **Examples:**
>
> on the table   against the grey rocks
>
> round the sharp bend   opposite him
>
> by your dog   after the game
>
>

Warm up

1 Find the noun phrase in each of these sentences.

a) The cat jumped.

b) Catch the red bus.

c) Poor Dorothy coughed.

d) The car broke down but the old van continued.

Test yourself

2 Copy and complete the following with one or two modifying adjectives to expand each noun phrase.

Example:

the **deep dark** wood

a) in the _____ garden
b) the _____ _____ shop
c) my _____ _____ classroom
d) a _____ _____ bedroom
e) our _____ _____ brother

Challenge yourself

3 Copy and expand these noun phrases by using a prepositional phrase.

a) The clever dog barked…
b) Alex watched TV…
c) The boys played…
d) Keira wore a dress…
e) The cat jumped…

4 Add an expanded noun phrase to complete these sentences.

a) We enjoy climbing up the hill towards…
b) The news reporter recorded the…
c) We enjoy playing outside in the…
d) The book is kept in the library…
e) The cricketer hit the ball to…

How did you do?

Progress test 1

1 Make a list of the **nouns** in the sentence below.

I rode on my bike while my cousin rode on his scooter.

2 Copy and complete the table below to show the singular and plural forms of each noun.

Singular	Plural
car	
	mice
knife	

The sentences below are incorrect. Rewrite them correctly.

3 The children was dancing.

4 Mike were laughing.

5 They was happy.

Is each word below singular or plural?

6 children

7 cat

8 men

9 Rewrite the sentence below correctly using an apostrophe.

Claudias legs were aching after running up the hill.

Progress test 1

Contract these words using an apostrophe.

10 they have

11 we are

12 he is

13 Rewrite this sentence with an apostrophe added.

The mens coats were all too big.

14 Identify the nouns in this sentence.

I like going to the library and choosing new books.

Copy and complete each sentence with either **did** or **done**.

15 What _____ you eat for your dinner?

16 We _____ well in the sports day.

For each pair of phrases below, draw pictures to show the meaning of both phrases.

17 the baby's hair   the babies' hair

18 the boy's skateboard   the boys' skateboards

Write a sentence using each of the following **prepositional phrases**.

19 before

20 on

Score ◯/20

Paragraphs

Paragraphs are used to help organise information in a text. They contain one or more sentences about an idea or topic.

In the writing of **fiction**, new paragraphs are used to:

- introduce new sections of a story
- introduce new characters
- introduce a new speaker of dialogue
- introduce a new theme
- show a change in time or place.

In the writing of **non-fiction**, paragraphs can sometimes start with a subheading and are used to:

- introduce new pieces of information
- introduce a new point of view
- organise ideas and facts clearly.

When writing, each paragraph should start on a new line. Paragraphs make the writing easier to read.

Warm up

1. Which of the following is a proper paragraph?

    a) Hair clip.

    b) I used my hair clip to pick the lock and escaped. Then I ran through the woods and hid.

    c) Nothing to drink.

Test yourself

2 a) Which statement below correctly describes a rule for paragraphs

   i) Paragraphs should contain at least two sentences.

   ii) Paragraphs should not contain more than ten sentences.

   iii) A new paragraph starts on a new line.

   iv) Paragraphs always have subheadings.

b) Explain how the rule you chose above is helpful to readers.

Challenge yourself

3 Read the story below, and decide where new paragraphs could start.

> One day the wind and the sun argued over which one was the strongest. Spotting a man travelling on the road, they decided to play a game to see which one could remove the jacket from the man's back the quickest. Of course, the wind thought he would win with no problem at all. How could the sun blow off the man's jacket? The wind began. He blew strong gusts of air, so strong that the man could barely walk against them. But the more the wind blew, the more the man pulled his jacket tight around him. The wind blew harder and stronger, but still the man pulled his jacket tighter and even fastened the buttons to keep himself warm. The wind blew until he was exhausted, but he could not remove the jacket from the man's back. It was now the sun's turn. He gently shone high in the sky. The sun did very little, but quietly shone down upon the man's back until the man became so warm that he took off his jacket and looked around for some shade.

How did you do?

Fronted Adverbials 1

An **adverbial phrase** is a group of words that act like an adverb, giving more information about **how**, **when**, **where** or **why** something is done.

Examples:

Clara jumped **into the water.** *(tells us **where**)*

We have been **at this school for five years**. *(tells us **where** and **when**)*

Fronted adverbials are when an adverb or adverbial phrase has been moved to the **beginning** of a sentence. They are used to create effect and make writing more interesting. A comma is used after a fronted adverbial.

Examples:

Carefully, the cat walked along the roof.

In 1948, they were married.

Warm up

1) Read the sentences below and find the adverbial phrases.

a) On Friday, I walked for half an hour.

b) I met my friends outside school.

c) I usually go and visit my grandma on a Wednesday.

d) Dan ate some chocolate after his tea.

e) Kosha practised playing the violin every day.

Test yourself

2) Read the sentences below and write whether the adverbial phrases are showing **where**, **when** or **how often** something happens. Some sentences may have more than one answer.

   a) I have a shower every day.

   b) My brother hid his homework under his bed.

   c) The dog barked when he went for a walk.

   d) I go to the library on a Wednesday afternoon.

   e) Our English lesson was in the hall.

Challenge yourself

3) Rewrite these sentences putting the adverb at the **front** of the sentence.

   a) The horse galloped quickly down the track.

   b) The bird darted swiftly through the sky.

   c) The little girl stroked the purring cat gently.

   d) The gymnast flew gracefully through the air.

4) Write four sentences of your own that include a fronted adverbial phrase.

How did you do?

Fronted Adverbials 2

When an adverbial phrase is used it can be written before or after the verb.
If it is written before the verb, it is called a **fronted adverbial**.

> **Examples:**
> **Yesterday afternoon**, he played tennis.
> **Later that day**, I went to the shops.

A comma should be used after the fronted adverbial.

Warm up

1) Copy these sentences. Underline the fronted adverbial and then add the missing comma.

   a) While I was asleep my brother played on the computer.

   b) In the morning I need to brush my teeth.

   c) Extremely loudly the band began to play.

   d) At the park Mohammed and Kai played on the swings.

   e) Quickly they ran to school.

2) Rewrite the sentences below but change the adverbial phrase to a fronted adverbial phrase. Remember to use a comma in the correct place.

   a) I ate an ice cream later that evening.

   b) The hospital was very busy after 4pm.

   c) The cat licked her fur while lying on the carpet.

   d) The swimmer entered the race with his sister.

   e) I like listening to stories at bedtime.

Answers

Pages 4–5
1. a) The <u>cows</u> were in the field.
   b) The excited <u>astronauts</u> were trying on their new <u>spacesuits</u>.
   c) We are going to the library to listen to <u>stories</u>.
   d) The <u>cats</u> and <u>dogs</u> were making lots of <u>noise</u> because they were frightened of the loud <u>fireworks</u>.
   e) We have <u>sandwiches</u>, <u>crisps</u>, <u>apples</u> and <u>sweets</u> in our picnic today.
   f) There were lots of <u>people</u> waiting at the platform for the next two <u>trains</u> this morning.
2. a) women   b) children
   c) teeth   d) feet
3. a) teacher   b) friends/teachers
   c) dogs, tails d) geese

Pages 6–7
1.

Full word	Contraction
can not	can't
would not	wouldn't
is not	isn't
you are	you're
we have	we've
I am	I'm
let us	let's
we are	we're
I will	I'll
they would / they had	they'd

2. a) Tom's jumper is too small for him.
   b) The giraffe's neck is very long.
   c) The men's toilets are out of order.
   d) This is Daniel's coat.
   e) Mrs Javaid's class are going on a school trip today.
   f) The girl's pencil case was green.
3. a) Accept any grammatically correct sentence using **it's**.
   b) Accept any grammatically correct sentence using **you've**.
   c) Accept any grammatically correct sentence using **didn't**.
   d) Accept any grammatically correct sentence using **I'll**.

Pages 8–9
1. a) were   b) was   c) was
   d) were   e) were   f) was
2. Once upon a time there **(a)** <u>was</u> a lion lying by a tree. A little mouse **(b)** <u>was</u> running up and down the lion's back and he **(c)** <u>was</u> beginning to make the lion angry. The lion turned its large head and opened its mouth widely. With its piercing eyes glaring, the lion **(d)** <u>was</u> about to swallow the little mouse in one big gulp. Just then the little mouse squeaked, "Please don't eat me! One day you might need me to help you."
The lion laughed but let the little mouse go free. He **(e)** <u>was</u> sure he would never need help from such a small pathetic creature.
Then, one day, three men **(f)** <u>were</u> walking through the forest holding nets. The men **(g)** <u>were</u> trying to catch the lion and swiftly threw a net over the lion's strong body. The lion roared and struggled but there **(h)** <u>was</u> nothing he could do. He could not escape.
Just then the little mouse returned to help the lion. He began, very slowly, to gnaw and chew through the net with his sharp teeth. Eventually, the mouse made a hole that **(i)** <u>was</u> wide enough for the lion to escape.
3. a) Were   b) Was
   c) Were   d) Was

Pages 10–11
1. a) did   b) done
   c) did   d) did
2. a) did   b) done   c) done
   d) Did   e) done   f) did
3. a) I have done all my homework!
   b) We did a handstand together.
   c) They did very well in their swimming lesson.
4. Accept any correct sentences using did and done.

Pages 12–13
1. verb
2. a) <u>My friend's cat</u> likes jumping.
   b) We ate dinner <u>in the kitchen</u>.
   c) I drank <u>a cup of warm tea</u>.
   d) Alex ran <u>along the beach</u>.
   e) <u>Kara's pink bedroom</u> was messy.
   f) He walked <u>down the path</u>.
   g) We can't go shopping <u>in the heavy rain</u>.
3. a) upside down
   b) of dirty plates
   c) small and quiet
   d) deep and cold
   e) at the park
   f) after lunch
4. a)–b) Accept any suitable and grammatically correct ending to the sentences.

Pages 14–15
1. a) <u>The cat</u> jumped.
   b) Catch <u>the red bus</u>.
   c) <u>Poor Dorothy</u> coughed.
   d) <u>The car</u> broke down but <u>the old van</u> continued.
2. Accept any suitable adjective, e.g.
   a) luscious, tidy, overgrown, small
   b) local, large, extensive, expensive
   c) tidy, organised, happy, quiet
   d) messy, relaxing, peaceful, tiny
   e) kind, annoying, little, brave
3. Accept any suitable prepositional phrase, e.g.
   a) The clever dog barked **in his basket**.
   b) Alex watched TV **on the sofa**.
   c) The boys played **next to the shops**.
   d) Keira wore a dress **after the ceremony**.
   e) The cat jumped **down the tree**.
4. Any suitable expanded noun phrase, e.g.
   a) We enjoy playing up the hill towards **our waving friends**.
   b) The news reporter recorded the **interview in front of the camera**.
   c) We enjoy playing outside in the **sunshine at the park**.
   d) The book is kept in the library **on the top shelf**.
   e) The cricketer hit the ball to **the other side of the pitch**.

Answers

Pages 16–17
1. bike, cousin, scooter
2. car = cars
   mouse = mice
   knife = knives
3. The children were dancing.
4. Mike was laughing.
5. They were happy.
6. children = plural
7. cat = singular
8. men = plural
9. Claudia's legs were aching after running up the hill.
10. they've
11. we're
12. he's
13. The men's coats were all too big.
14. library, books
15. What **did** you eat for your dinner?
16. We **did** well in the sports day.
17. Picture showing one baby with hair / Picture showing several babies with hair
18. Picture showing one boy with skateboard / Picture showing several boys with several skateboards
    Any sentence which uses the phrases and makes sense, e.g.
19. I went to the shops before school.
20. Please don't write on the table.

Pages 18–19
1. b) I used my hair clip to pick the lock and escaped. Then I ran through the woods and hid.
2. a) A new paragraph starts on a new line.
   b) It makes the writing easier to follow / read.
3. **Paragraphs can be made as follows, though not all of them are necessary:**
   One day the wind and the sun argued over which one was the strongest.
   Spotting a man travelling on the road, they decided to play a game to see which one could remove the jacket from the man's back the quickest.
   Of course, the wind thought he would win with no problem at all. How could the sun blow off the man's jacket?
   The wind began. He blew strong gusts of air, so strong that the man could barely walk against them. But the more the wind blew, the more the man pulled his jacket tight around him. The wind blew harder and stronger, but still the man pulled his jacket tighter and even fastened the buttons to keep himself warm. The wind blew until he was exhausted, but he could not remove the jacket from the man's back.
   It was now the sun's turn. He gently shone high in the sky. The sun did very little, but quietly shone down upon the man's back until the man became so warm that he took off his jacket and looked around for some shade.

Pages 20–21
1. a) <u>On Friday,</u> I walked <u>for half an hour</u>.
   b) I met my friends <u>outside school</u>.
   c) I <u>usually</u> go and visit my grandma <u>on a Wednesday</u>.
   d) Dan ate some chocolate <u>after his tea</u>.
   e) Kosha practised playing the violin <u>every day</u>.
2. a) how often b) where c) when
   d) where and when e) where
3. **Accept any suitable answer.**
   a) Quickly, the horse galloped down the track.
   b) Swiftly, the bird darted through the sky.
   c) Gently, the little girl stroked the purring cat.
   d) Gracefully, the gymnast flew through the air.
4. **Accept any sentence that makes sense and starts with a fronted adverbial, e.g.:** Eagerly, the geese pecked at the bread.

Pages 22–23
1. a) <u>While I was asleep,</u> my brother played on the computer.
   b) <u>In the morning,</u> I need to brush my teeth.
   c) <u>Extremely loudly,</u> the band began to play.
   d) <u>At the park,</u> Mohammed and Kai played on the swings.
   e) <u>Quickly,</u> they ran to school.
2. a) Later that evening, I ate an ice cream.
   b) After 4pm, the hospital was very busy.
   c) While lying on the carpet, the cat licked her fur.
   d) With his sister, the swimmer entered the race.
   e) At bedtime, I like listening to stories.
3. **Any suitable adverbial phrase, e.g.**
   a) Slowly, Carefully, Quietly
   b) At midnight, Very loudly, When I was still asleep
   c) At night, In the morning, While everyone was busy
   d) Quickly, Slowly, Feeling happy
   e) Before bed, Yesterday morning, At the library
   f) On Thursday, After school, While I was at work
   g) Last year, During the school holidays, When I was seven
   h) Proudly, Finally, This morning
4. **Any correct sentences using a fronted adverbial with a comma afterwards, e.g.**
   When I was outside, I heard a bird singing.

Pages 24–25
1. he, their, she, it, I, our
2. a) Charlie was tired so <u>he</u> went upstairs to <u>his</u> bedroom.
   b) A large, black spider crawled up <u>my</u> arm when <u>I</u> was not looking!
   c) Rebecca played with <u>our</u> toys while <u>we</u> were on holiday.
   d) <u>My</u> sister, Bethan, doesn't eat many sweets because <u>she</u> knows <u>they</u> are bad for <u>her</u> teeth.
   e) The builder came to <u>our</u> house but <u>we</u> were out.
   f) "I loved the show. <u>It</u> was great!" <u>he</u> said.
3. An old man on the point of death called **his** sons to give them some advice. He told them to bring in a bundle of sticks, and said to the eldest son: "Break it."
   The son really strained, but was unable to break the bundle. The other sons tried too, but none of **them** could do it.
   "Untie the bundle," said the father, "and each of **you** take a stick."
   When **they** each had a stick, he said to them: "Now, break them," and each stick broke easily. "You see what I mean?" said **their** father.
4. Dexter read a long book even though **he** found **it** difficult.

Pages 26–27
1. it, their, her, our, his, they, mine
2. a) Preta ate a sandwich. **It** was delicious.
   b) Eliza danced for ages at the disco. **Her** legs ached when **it** had finished.
   c) Mum asked us to put our shoes on, but **they** were dirty.
   d) My aunt has a dog. **It's** called Maple and it's **her** best friend.

2

Answers

e) We went to the fair. **It** was lots of fun because we went on lots of rides. Sarah came with us too. **She** ate lots of candy floss.
f) The teachers told us about the school trip. **They** said we need to bring lots of things.
g) My recorder isn't working properly. When I play **it**, it keeps making funny sounds and I hate **it**!
h) Tobias watched a great film even though **it** made **him** feel a little bit scared!

3. Today the weather will be warm and dry. **It** will start cloudy in most areas of England and Wales but by lunchtime, **it** will be warmer and the sun will be shining!
Today is a day for being outside! Devon and Cornwall will see the highest temperatures. **They** will also have the least likelihood of any rain.
Unfortunately, in the North, Lincolnshire and Yorkshire may see some rain showers overnight and **they** will have some cool temperatures after midnight.

4. At Paige's birthday party, there was a clever magician who waved his wand gently over a special box. **He** shouted the magic words three times and then **he** clapped his hands. The magician asked Paige to choose a helper from the audience. **She** didn't know who to choose so in the end **she** chose me, Sam. **I** went to the front of the stage and helped the magician mysteriously produce a white rabbit. Everyone in the audience thought the trick was brilliant; **they** loved the trick and **they** loved the rabbit too!

Pages 28–29
1. a) The people, who were waiting at the bus stop, wanted the next bus to be red.
   b) An artist, who painted in the style of Van Gogh, once entered his work in an exhibition.
   c) A local choir beat a flautist, a clarinettist and a pianist to win first prize at the National Music Festival.
2. He wanted to buy a new car.
3. a) Although **the** tide was coming in, we still managed to have some time playing on **the / a** beach.
   b) On Saturday **the** weather will be humid with **a** thunderstorm likely.
   c) Mum asked us to shut **the** windows because **the** rain was coming in.
   d) **An / The** African elephant has larger ears than **an / the** Asian elephant.
   e) Our class went on **a / the** visit to **a / the** science museum in London.
   f) My sister screamed when she saw **a / the** large, hairy spider crawl across her bedroom.

Pages 30–31
1. Any two from the following:
   – to introduce a new character
   – to introduce a new place / setting
   – to move to a new event
   – to move a story on in time
   – to organise information
   – to make it clearer for the reader.
2. A spider
3. An ant
4. Jake and **I** watched his dad wash the car.
5. "You splashed **me**," I shouted.
6. she
7. An aeroplane landed at London Gatwick after a seven hour delay.
8. Michael's test results were disappointing. He felt sad that they were not better.
9. Luisa ran so fast her legs were aching and she felt exhausted.
10. comma
11. Later that morning, the children walked to the bus stop.
12. Without thinking, the little girl gave her sparkling fairy wings to her friend.
13. an egg, a ball, the cows
    Any sentence that makes sense, e.g.
14. Back at the house, Jonah played on his computer.
15. While I was waiting, I read a magazine.
16. Once a week, we go shopping.
17. Mrs Taylor liked her class. They were lovely.
18. The tennis player won a tournament. She / He won a silver trophy.
19. Do you like Alice's new bike? It is red. She loves it.
20. The dog was barking so it's/his/her owner ran over to it/he/her.

Pages 32–33
1. a) "Can you write me a shopping list?" Mum asked.
   b) The teacher shouted, "I'm waiting for you to listen."
   c) The doctor said, "Take a seat, please."
   d) "What music do you like listening to?" my friends asked.
   e) "I'm hungry Mum. When is dinner ready?"
   f) Mum replied, "It will be ready in ten minutes."
2. a) "Where are you going on holiday?" asked our neighbour.
   b) "What time does school start?"
   c) "Can we bake a cake this afternoon?" Brooke asked.
   d) "Help!" my brother shouted.
   e) "I need some new trainers because mine have holes in," I told my dad.
   f) The head teacher stated, "All ball games must be played outside."
   g) The librarian whispered, "Please do not eat or drink in the library."
   h) "What colour is your tennis racket?" my friends asked.
3. **Accept any vocabulary that makes sense – check inverted commas and punctuation are correct.**
   a) I will win the race easily. I am much faster than you!" the Hare said.
   "We'll see about that!" the Tortoise replied.
   b) "Little pigs, little pigs, let me come in," the Wolf shouted.
   "No you can't come in!" the Pigs shouted back.
   "Then I'll huff and I'll puff and I'll blow your house down," threatened the Wolf.
   c) "Feeding time for the penguins will be at 2 p.m." the zookeeper told the visitors.
   "Are we allowed to take photographs?" the boy asked.
   d) "I've lost my purse," the little girl mumbled sadly.
   "Did you have a lot of money in it?" the police officer asked.
   "No, not really," the little girl replied.

Pages 34–35
1. a) "I love going to school," Ben said.
   b) "The train is delayed, so I'm going to be home late," Dad grumbled.
   c) "Can you tell me where the nearest shop is, please?"
   d) "Ouch!" Mrs Baker shouted. "I've hurt my toe!"
2. a) "Hurry up! You'll be late!" Mum yelled up the stairs.
   "I'm coming!" I replied.
   b) "Hello. How can I help you?" the doctor asked.
   "I have a nasty cough and a very sore throat," I replied.

Answers

c) "What would you like in your lunch box tomorrow?" Dad asked.
"Please can I have ham sandwiches with tomatoes and crisps?" I answered.
"Of course you can."
d) "Has everyone got a piece of paper?" Mr Evans asked.
"I haven't," I said.
"Don't worry. I will get you one," he replied.
3. "What time are you leaving?" I asked my friends.
"We will be going at about two o'clock," they replied.
"Can I come too?" I asked.
"Of course you can."

Page 36–37

1.

Standard English	Non-standard English
Thank you very much.	It was dead nice.
I am happy with my work.	You're well cool.
The flowers are beautiful.	I did a good story.
Someone smiled at me.	I been bad.
	I've not got none.

2. a) I have not done anything wrong. / I have done nothing wrong.
   b) They were laughing at us.
   c) I am not happy.
   d) They should not/shouldn't have run away.
   e) I do not/don't like those sweets.
3. She were naughty is non-standard English.
   That ain't good is non-standard English.
   I did not see anything is standard English.
   They went to the seaside is standard English.
   I isn't going anywhere is non-standard English.
   This is the picture that I made is standard English.

Pages 38–39

1. a) I am going to go to After School Club today.
   b) The farmer has lots of animals in his field.
   c) We are going to the seaside tomorrow. I am looking forward to it.
2. **Accept any suitable sentences that use an exclamation mark and are grammatically correct, e.g.**
   a) Ouch! I have hurt my finger!
   b) Stop it! Please don't argue anymore!
   c) Help! Help! I'm stuck in the lift!
3. a) Please can someone help me?
   b) Would you like to go to the playground today?
   c) Where is the train station?
4. a) I am going to play outside in the snow.
   b) Where are my shoes? I can't find them anywhere.
   c) Are you ready for the race tomorrow?

Pages 40–41

1. a) **E**very **W**ednesday, there is a half price sale on all fizzy soft drinks.
   b) Fireworks can only be **sold** to people over the age of 21/twenty one.
   c) Are you ready for the summer? There is 50% off our bbq/barbecue selection.
   d) If you **take** your till receipt to the information desk, we will give you a free ticket for the car park.
   e) Sorry! We have **sold** out of pizzas today.
   f) **M**ay madness! **B**uy three bags of fruit and only pay **for** two!

2. **Any four different features of grammar and punctuation, e.g.:**
   full stops, capital letters, commas, spelling, verb agreement, use of pronouns, tense agreement, use of conjunctions, question marks, inverted commas
3. a) Once upon a time, there was a little boy called Sam who lived out on a farm far away from any other children. He lived only with his mother and father who were often busy and the boy usually felt lonely and sad.
   b) One day, he was playing in the garden when he saw another boy, about his age, walk past his garden. He felt very excited and ran straight over and said, "Hello, what's your name?"
   c) "My name is Alin," the little boy replied. "I am walking to the market in the main village."
   "Can I come with you?" Sam asked.
   "Of course you can; we can be friends."

Pages 42–43

1. Sophie won second place in the skipping race at sports day. She was very happy.
2. I love gardening with my sister at the weekend. We are trying to grow some vegetables of our own.
3. Speech marks
4. "Can you hear me?" I asked.
5. "Can I go and play at Al's house?" I asked Dad.
6. "Yes, but make sure you are home for 5pm," Dad replied.
7. Speedy went so fast on his skateboard he overtook a bicycle.
   Any correct example, e.g.
8. a letter of complaint, a letter to someone regarding work, a letter to thank someone for something, to someone unknown
9. to a friend inviting them to a party, to a family member via email
10. I love watching football. It's very good.
11. b) The teacher shouted, "Please sit down!"
12. **Any suitable question ending in a question mark, e.g.**
    When is your birthday?
13. "Can I stay up late to watch TV Mum?" James asked.
14. "No, because it's a school night, but you can stay up later at the weekend," James's mum replied.
15. **Accept any suitable exclamation, e.g.** I can't believe it!
16. What do you want for tea?
17. I will be late home tonight because I am going to stay at school for choir.
18. 7pm – all children needed at dress rehearsal
19. **Any correct example, e.g.** People often go to the beach on holiday.
20. **Any correct example, e.g.** email, story, newspaper report etc.

Test yourself

3 Copy and complete these sentences. Write fronted adverbial phrases at the start of each one. Remember to use a comma after the adverbial!

a) _____ the mouse nibbled the cheese.

b) _____ the gun went off.

c) _____ the cat prowled the garden.

d) _____ he crossed the finishing line.

e) _____ he read a book.

f) _____ he took his skateboard to the park.

g) _____ we went on holiday.

h) _____ the teacher praised the class.

Challenge yourself

4 Write **four** sentences of your own that include a fronted adverbial phrase.

Remember to add the comma in the correct place.

How did you do?

23

Pronouns 1

A **pronoun** is a word that is used to replace a noun. Pronouns are often used so that the noun is not repeated and to make our writing more interesting.

Example:

noun: **Tom** plays the piano. pronoun: **He** practises every day.

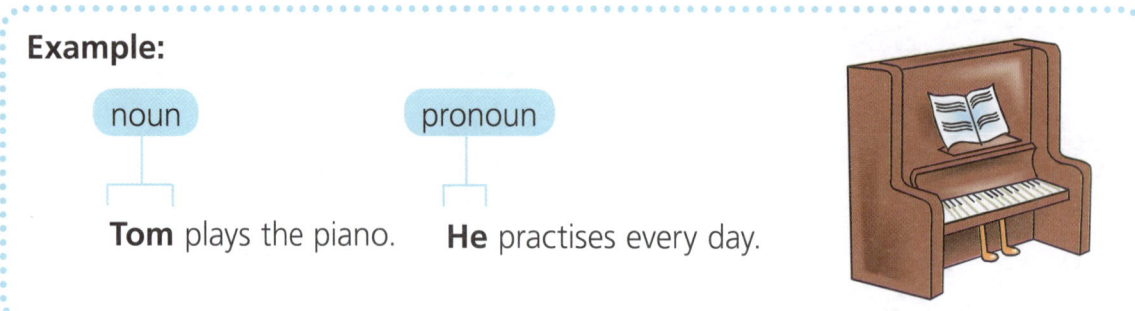

Some common pronouns are:

Examples:

I, me, my, mine	it, its
you, your, yours	we, us, our, ours
he, him, his	they, them, their, theirs
she, her, hers	

Warm up

1 Write down the words below that are pronouns.

he	their	cat	Mrs
Matthew	walking	John	car
she	it	chair	I
house	Sophia	our	snake

Test yourself

2 Identify the pronouns in each sentence.

a) Charlie was tired so he went upstairs to his bedroom.

b) A large, black spider crawled up my arm when I was not looking!

c) Rebecca played with our toys while we were on holiday.

d) My sister, Bethan, doesn't eat many sweets because she knows they are bad for her teeth.

e) The builder came to our house but we were out.

f) "I loved the show. It was great!" he said.

Challenge yourself

3 Choose the correct pronoun below to fill each of the gaps in the story.

his	them	they	you	their

An old man on the point of death called **(a)** _____ sons to give them some advice. He told them to bring in a bundle of sticks, and said to the eldest son:

"Break it."

The son really strained, but was unable to break the bundle. The other sons tried too, but none of **(b)** _____ could do it.

"Untie the bundle," said the father, "and each of **(c)** _____ take a stick."

When **(d)** _____ each had a stick, he said to them:

"Now, break them," and each stick broke easily. "You see what I mean?" said

(e) _____ father.

4 Rewrite the sentence below, replacing the words in bold with a pronoun.

Dexter read a long book even though **Dexter** found **the long book** difficult.

How did you do?

Pronouns 2

Remember that using pronouns makes your writing less repetitive and more interesting for the reader.

Warm up

1 Write down the words below that are pronouns.

Pueblo	it	their	her
fish	holiday	our	wedding	his
they	castle	Japan	mine	and

Test yourself

2 Rewrite these sentences replacing the words in bold with a correct pronoun.

a) Preta ate a sandwich. **The sandwich** was delicious.

b) Eliza danced for ages at the disco. **Eliza's** legs ached when **the disco** had finished.

c) Mum asked us to put our shoes on, but **the shoes** were dirty.

d) My aunt has a dog. **The dog** is called Maple and it's **my aunt's** best friend.

e) We went to the fair. **The fair** was lots of fun because we went on lots of rides. Sarah came with us too. **Sarah** ate lots of candyfloss.

f) The teachers told us about the school trip. **The teachers** said we need to bring lots of things.

g) My recorder isn't working properly. When I play **the recorder**, it keeps making funny sounds and I hate **the recorder**!

h) Tobias watched a great film even though **the film** made **Tobias** feel a little bit scared!

Challenge yourself

3 Read this weather report. Which nouns could be changed to pronouns to make the report easier to understand?

> Today the weather will be warm and dry. The weather will start cloudy in most areas of England and Wales but by lunchtime, the weather will be warmer and the sun will be shining!
>
> Today is a day for being outside! In the south, Devon and Cornwall will see the highest temperatures. Devon and Cornwall will also have the least likelihood of any rain.
>
> Unfortunately, in the north, Lincolnshire and Yorkshire may see some rain showers overnight and Lincolnshire and Yorkshire will have some cool temperatures after midnight.
>
>

4 Read the passage below. Which nouns could be changed to pronouns to make the story easier to understand?

> At Paige's birthday party, there was a clever magician who waved his wand gently over a special box. The magician shouted the magic words three times and then the magician clapped his hands. The magician asked Paige to choose a helper from the audience. Paige didn't know who to choose so in the end Paige chose me, Sam. Sam went to the front of the stage and helped the magician mysteriously produce a white rabbit. Everyone in the audience thought the trick was brilliant; the audience loved the trick and the audience loved the rabbit too!
>
>

How did you do?

Determiners and articles

A **determiner** goes before a noun or noun phrase. The most common determiners are **the**, **a** and **an**. They are also known as **articles**.

The **definite article** is **the**. It is normally used when we are talking about a particular thing.

> **Examples:**
>
> **the** piano   **the** egg   **the** new school

The **indefinite** article is **a** or **an**. These are normally used when we are talking about a thing in general.

> **Examples:**
>
> **a** piano   **an** egg   **a** new school

We use **a** before a word beginning with a consonant and **an** before a word beginning with a vowel. Words beginning with a silent **h** are exceptions. We use **an** before them because they have a vowel sound.

> **Examples:**
>
> **a** hospital (**h** is not silent)   **an** hour (**h** is silent)

Warm up

1) Identify the **determiners** in each sentence below.

   a) The people, who were waiting at the bus stop, wanted the next bus to be red.

   b) An artist, who painted in the style of Van Gogh, once entered his work in an exhibition.

   c) A local choir beat a flautist, a clarinettist and a pianist to win first prize at the National Music Festival.

28

Test yourself

2 Which sentence uses the correct **determiner**?

a) We eat the cake every day.

b) A octopus has eight legs.

c) She travels into the London every day for work.

d) He wanted to buy a new car.

Challenge yourself

3 Choose **a**, **an** or **the** to fill in the gaps in the sentences below.

a) Although _____ tide was coming in, we still managed to have some time playing on _____ beach.

b) On Saturday _____ weather will be humid with _____ thunderstorm likely.

c) Mum asked us to shut _____ windows because _____ rain was coming in.

d) _____ African elephant has larger ears than _____ Asian elephant.

e) Our class went on _____ visit to _____ science museum in London.

f) My sister screamed when she saw _____ large, hairy spider crawl across her bedroom.

How did you do?

Progress test 2

1 Give two reasons why a new paragraph should be started.

Copy and write **a** or **an** before each noun.

2 spider

3 ant

Copy and add the pronouns **I** and **me** to the sentences below to make them correct.

4 Jake and _____ watched his dad wash the car.

5 "You splashed _____," I shouted.

6 Which **pronoun** from the given words would you choose to complete the sentence?

| her   she   we   it   me |

Aisha went to the shops and _____ bought some ice cream.

7 Copy and circle the determiners in the sentence below.

An aeroplane landed at London Gatwick after a seven hour delay.

Copy and complete these sentences using suitable pronouns.

8 Michael's test results were disappointing. _____ felt sad that _____ were not better.

9 Luisa ran so fast _____ legs were aching and _____ felt exhausted.

Progress test 2

10) Which type of punctuation is used after a fronted adverbial?

   a) full stop

   b) comma

   c) apostrophe

   d) exclamation mark

Identify the fronted adverbial in each of the sentences below.

11) Later that morning, the children walked to the bus stop.

12) Without thinking, the little girl gave her sparkling fairy wings to her friend.

13) Look at the determiners below. Which ones are correct?

a children   an elephants   an egg   a ball   the cows   an chip

The sentences below all start with a fronted adverbial. Complete each sentence. Remember to punctuate them correctly.

14) Back at the house…

15) While I was waiting…

16) Once a week…

Rewrite these sentences using suitable pronouns.

17) Mrs Taylor liked Mrs Taylor's class. The class was lovely.

18) The tennis player won a tournament. The tennis player won a silver trophy.

19) Do you like Alice's new bike? The new bike is red. Alice loves the new bike.

20) The dog was barking so the dog's owner ran over to the dog.

Score ◯ / 20

Direct speech 1

Direct speech is what a speaker actually says. When we write, inverted commas are used to show where the direct speech begins and ends.

If the sentence begins with direct speech, we add a comma, exclamation mark or question mark just before the inverted comma at the end.

Example:

"Make sure you tidy your bedroom please," Mum reminded us.

If the sentence begins by telling us who is speaking, a comma should appear before the speech begins. When the direct speech finishes, it should normally end with a comma, question mark or exclamation mark just before the inverted comma at the end.

Example:

Mum shouted up the stairs, "Remember to tidy your bedroom please."

Inverted commas are sometimes also called speech marks.

Warm up

1. Copy and add inverted commas around what is being said below.

   a) Can you write me a shopping list? Mum asked.

   b) The teacher shouted, I'm waiting for you to listen.

   c) The doctor said, Take a seat, please.

d) What music do you like listening to? my friends asked.

e) I'm hungry Mum. When is dinner ready?

f) Mum replied, It will be ready in ten minutes.

Test yourself

2) Copy the sentences below and put inverted commas and punctuation in the correct places.

a) Where are you going on holiday asked our neighbour

b) What time does school start

c) Can we bake a cake this afternoon Brooke asked

d) Help my brother shouted

e) I need some new trainers because mine have holes in I told my dad

f) The head teacher stated All ball games must be played outside

g) The librarian whispered Please do not eat or drink in the library

h) What colour is your tennis racket my friends asked

Challenge yourself

3) Look at the playscripts below. Rewrite these as conversations using inverted commas and the correct punctuation.

a) The Hare: I will win the race easily. I am much faster than you!
The Tortoise: We'll see about that.

b) Wolf: Little pigs, little pigs, let me come in.
Pigs: No, you can not come in.
Wolf: Then I'll huff and I'll puff and I'll blow your house down.

c) Zookeeper: Feeding time for the penguins will be at 2 p.m.
Boy: Are we allowed to take photographs?

d) Little girl: I've lost my purse.
Police officer: Did you have a lot of money in it?
Little girl: No, not really.

How did you do?

Direct speech 2

In a conversation between two or more people, when a new person starts speaking, the speech is written on a **new line**.

Examples:

"Please can I have some new rollerblades?" I asked my mum hopefully.

Mum replied, "You will have to wait until it is your birthday."

"But that is ages away!"

"You could save your pocket money," Mum suggested, "and buy some yourself."

Notice that all direct speech starts with a **capital letter**, except where the sentence of direct speech is broken by information about who is talking.

Warm up

1 Copy these sentences and put inverted commas around what is being said.

a) I love going to school, Ben said.

b) The train is delayed, so I'm going to be home late, Dad grumbled.

c) Can you tell me where the nearest shop is please?

d) Ouch! Mrs Baker shouted. I've hurt my toe!

Test yourself

2) Rewrite these conversations using inverted commas and the correct punctuation. Remember to start a new line for each new speaker.

a) Hurry up You'll be late Mum yelled up the stairs I'm coming I replied

b) Hello How can I help you the doctor asked I have a nasty cough and a very sore throat I replied

c) What would you like in your lunch box tomorrow Dad asked Please can I have ham sandwiches with tomatoes and crisps I answered Of course you can.

d) Has everyone got a piece of paper Mr Evans asked I haven't I said Don't worry I will get you one he replied.

Challenge yourself

3) Copy these sentences and add inverted commas and the correct punctuation. Remember to start a new line when a new person starts speaking.

What time are you leaving I asked my friends We will be going at about two o'clock they replied Can I come too I asked Of course you can

How did you do?

35

Standard and non-standard English

Standard English is generally formal English that contains correct grammar and punctuation with a range of sentence types.

Non-standard English often uses incorrect grammar and punctuation and is very informal. It is usually slang or colloquial language. Non-standard English reflects many people's spoken English and is not really used in written English except for the most informal writing.

Warm up

1 Copy the table below and write the sentences in either the **standard** or **non-standard English** column.

It was dead nice. You're well cool. Thank you very much.

I did a good story. I am happy with my work. I been bad.

The flowers are beautiful. Someone smiled at me. I've not got none.

Standard English	Non-standard English

Test yourself

2 Rewrite each sentence below in **standard English**.

a) I not done nothing wrong.

b) They was laughing at us.

c) I isn't happy.

d) They shouldn't of ran away.

e) I don't like them sweets.

Challenge yourself

3 Which of these sentences use standard English and which use non-standard English?

She were naughty.

That ain't good.

I did not see anything.

They went to the seaside.

I isn't going anywhere.

This is the picture that I made.

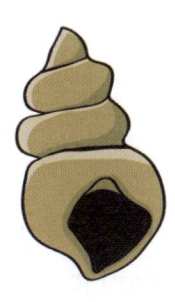

How did you do?

Full stops, Exclamation marks and Questions marks

Most sentences end with a **full stop**.

> **Examples:**
>
> Tom went into the library to borrow a book.
>
> This morning, I decided to bake a cake. I had to go to the shops to buy the ingredients.

An **exclamation mark** can be used at the end of a command to show it is urgent.

> **Examples:**
>
> Go away!
>
> Quick, run!

An exclamation mark can also be used at the end of a sentence to show emotion, such as happiness, excitement, pain or anger.

> **Examples:**
>
> How wonderful!
>
> That's a disgrace!

A **question mark** is used at the end of a sentence when a question is being asked. A question mark is used instead of a full stop.

> **Example:**
>
> Are you ready to order?

Warm up

1 Read the sentences below and put full stops in the correct places.

a) I am going to go to After School Club today

b) The farmer has lots of animals in his field

c) We are going to the seaside tomorrow I am looking forward to it

Test yourself

2 Look at the exclamations and write a sentence using each one. Do not forget to include an exclamation mark.

> **Example: Oh, no!**
> Oh, no! My toast is burnt!

a) Ouch!

b) Stop it!

c) Help!

3 Copy the questions below. Put a question mark in the correct place for each one.

a) Please can someone help me

b) Would you like to go to the playground today

c) Where is the train station

Challenge yourself

4 Copy the sentences below. Decide which ones are questions and which ones are statements and then put either a full stop or a question mark in the correct place.

a) I am going to play outside in the snow

b) Where are my shoes I can't find them anywhere

c) Are you ready for the race tomorrow

How did you do?

Proof reading

It is important to check written work for spelling and punctuation mistakes. This is called 'proof reading'.

It is sometimes helpful to use a checklist when proof reading.

Example:

I have checked	Tick	I have checked	Tick
Capital letters are used correctly.		Any speech is correctly punctuated	
Sentences end with either a full stop, question mark or exclamation mark.		Words are written in the correct tense.	

Warm up

1 Look at these examples of notices at a supermarket. Rewrite each one correctly without the mistake/s.

a) every wednesday there is a half price sale on all fizzy soft drinks.

b) Fireworks can only be selled to people over the age of 21

c) Are you ready for the summer   There is 50% off our bbq selection.

d) If you taked your till receipt to the information desk we will give you a free ticket for the car park.

e) Sorry! We have selled out of pizzas today.

f) may madness! buy three bags of fruit and only pay four two

Test yourself

2 Copy and complete a proof reading checklist.

Write four things that you might check writing for when you are proof reading.

I have checked	Tick

Challenge yourself

3 Look at the passages below. Rewrite them correcting any mistakes you notice.

a) Once upon a time there was a little boy called Sam who lived out on a farm far away from any other children he lived only with his mother and father who were often busy and the boy usually felt lonely and sad

b) one day he was playing in the garden when he saw another boy, about his age walk past his garden he felt very excited and ran straight over and said hello what's your name

c) my name is alin the little boy replied I am walking to the market in the main village.

Can I come with you sam asked

Of course you can; we can be friends.

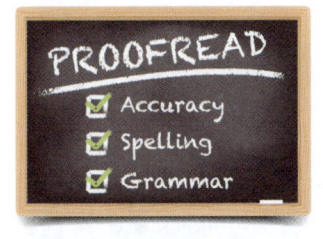

PROOFREAD
- Accuracy
- Spelling
- Grammar

How did you do?

Progress test 3

Rewrite the sentences below adding any full stops or capital letters in the correct place.

1. sophie won second prize in the skipping race at sports day she was very happy

2. i love gardening with my sister at the weekend we are trying to grow some vegetables of our own

3. What is another name for inverted commas?

    a) commas

    b) exclamation marks

    c) inverted full stops

    d) speech marks

4. Copy the sentence below and add inverted commas in the correct place.

    Can you hear me? I asked.

Copy the conversations below and add the inverted commas and correct punctuation.

5. Can I go and play at Al's house I asked Dad

6. Yes but make sure you are home for 5pm Dad replied.

7. Copy the sentence below. Add any missing full stops or capital letters.

    speedy went so fast on his skateboard he overtook a bicycle

Give an example of when you might be asked to write a letter that uses:

8. standard English

9. non-standard English

10. Rewrite this sentence using standard English.

    I love watching football, it's well good.

Progress test 3

11 Which sentence uses inverted commas correctly?

   a) "The teacher shouted please sit down!"

   b) The teacher shouted, "Please sit down!"

   c) The teacher shouted, Please "Sit down!"

   d) "The teacher shouted," please sit down.

12 Write a sentence that uses a question mark.

Turn the sentences below into a dialogue between the two characters. Remember to use inverted commas and speech punctuation correctly.

13 James is going to ask his mum if he can stay up late to watch TV.

14 James's mum is going to say no because it is a school night but he can stay up later at the weekend.

15 Write an exclamation.

Rewrite these text messages in standard English.

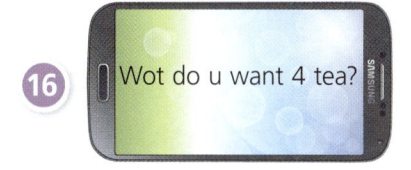

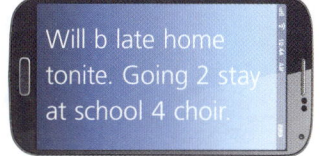

16 Wot do u want 4 tea?

17 Will b late home tonite. Going 2 stay at school 4 choir.

18 Rewrite this message in informal English.

   Please can all children attend a dress rehearsal on Monday evening at 7.00 pm.

19 Write a statement.

20 Give one example of a type of text where you may find direct speech.

Score ◯/20

43

Published by Keen Kite Books
An imprint of HarperCollins*Publishers* Ltd
The News Building
1 London Bridge Street
London SE1 9GF

ISBN 9780008161392

Text and Design © 2015 Keen Kite Books, an imprint of HarperCollins*Publishers* Ltd

Author: Laura Griffiths

The author asserts their moral right to be identified as the author of this work.

All rights reserved. No part of this publication may be reproduced, stored in a retrieval system, or transmitted, in any form or by any means, electronic, mechanical, photocopying, recording or otherwise, without the prior permission of Keen Kite Books.